THE
MILLION DOLLAR
METHOD

"If you are looking for a fresh vision to lead your company, organization, or ministry through the challenges and opportunities ahead, you've picked up the right book. The inspiring stories and practical application Jerod offers will ignite hope for what God can do through you and for those you serve. And here is the most incredible information about this reading adventure; you will glean insight on funding the vision! Yes, Jerod has raised millions of dollars for feeding the hungry, clean water projects, building schools and churches, and so much more. If you, like me, need more resources to fund the vision, you must hear what Jerod has to say."

—**Rodney Fouts**
Lead Pastor of North Church

"I love what Jerod has provided in the way of vision and approach in this book! One of the honors of my life has been the opportunity to coach and sponsor pastors who are planting new churches. 'The challenge and skill of casting vision and raising friends and funds is one of the biggest learning curves for planters. This resource will be a tremendous benefit to everyone."

—Jeff Leake
Lead Pastor of Allison Park Church
Author of *Gateway To A Supernatural Life*

"If you're reading this book, God has given you a vision. He's burdened your heart to serve others through your nonprofit. He's also been preparing people with the resources to fund your mission. Jerod Smith has encapsulated his common-sense, time-proven, and high-impact method for raising millions of dollars in these pages. Sow into your ministry by reading his newest book—*The Million Dollar Method*—and reap the benefits of his experience."

—Martijn van Tilborgh
Founder of Four Rivers Media and Co-Founder of AVAIL

"Jerod Smith is a missionary, entrepreneur, and coach, who lives a life of selfless compassion. Through his years of experience, he has learned the art of developing fundraising strategies that have made way for countless lives to be changed. He took all this knowledge and put it in a book to help leaders be more effective in raising the funds they need. *The Million Dollar Method* is a book for any church, leader, nonprofit organization, or missionary, who is looking for proven strategies to grow and add value to their work."

—Dr. Mike Burnette
Lead pastor of Lifepoint Church in Clarksville, TN

"My friend Jerod Smith has a special calling on his life–to help other ministry and marketplace leaders raise capital for their vision. This book is pure gold for those raising money continuously for their vision fulfillment. You and your teams will learn, grow, and most of all help others grow. Some call it 'fund-raising', but as Jerod will explain it is much more than that."

—**Sam Chand**
Leadership Consultant and Author of *Leadership Pain*

Cover design by Sara Young
Cover photo by Jim Felder Photography

ISBN: 978-1-959095-78-1   1 2 3 4 5 6 7 8 9 10

Printed in the United States of America

THE
MILLION DOLLAR METHOD

THE PROVEN STRATEGY THAT WILL RAISE
MILLIONS FOR YOUR NONPROFIT OR BUSINESS

JEROD M. SMITH

**DREAM
RELEASER
PUBLISHING**

This book is dedicated to Jesus, my family, and the many faithful donors that I've had the privilege to work with. Both have taught me so much and extended me more grace than I deserve.

Shanelle,

Go raise Millions!

CONTENTS

INTRODUCTION

A s we exited the aircraft, we were quickly met by the warm, moistureless air of Rwanda's dry season. This was our first missionary appointment, and transitioning from the United States with my wife, Katina, and our nine-year-old son to one of Africa's most war-torn countries with only seventeen trunks of our belongings was the most significant undertaking of our lives. It took about five minutes to realize that the life we had grown accustomed to was over. The foreign would have to become familiar.

Disembarking the plane, walking across the tarmac, clearing customs, collecting our baggage, and finding our contact were completely different. Not just different. Stressful. In fact, I remember the crippling doubt that made me secretly whisper, *What have I done?*

It took over six months to find a place to live. In the meantime, we lived in another missionary family's house while they were home on leave. Setting up a post office box, obtaining a green card, and adjusting to social customs were much more complex than we had ever imagined, but the Rwandan people were accommodating in their help to get us settled. It was this gracious spirit that helped us quickly fall in love with the Rwandan people.

Over the next several years, we served as frontline missionaries, helping to share the gospel with people who had suffered one of the worst genocides in history. The Rwandan genocide against the Tutsi brought the death of roughly one million people.

"We are rebuilding the country from scratch," one friend in the government told me.

Imagine every public system—all infrastructure—destroyed in a country. Government, education, banking, healthcare, and even places of worship were just gone—along with those who were working to keep them running. Even though the racial tensions had begun many years prior, the process of bringing Rwanda to ground zero only took one hundred days in 1994.

Imagine every public system—all infrastructure—destroyed in a country. Government, education, banking, healthcare, and even places of worship were just gone—along with those who were working to keep them running.

As the years went by, we learned how to be missionaries, planning outreaches, making inroads with the Rwandan people, and designing strategies to do our part to rebuild Rwanda for the better. If it were not for special people like Pastor Everest and his wife, Annette, our Rwandan pastors, we may have returned to the US defeated in the first year. However, with their mentoring and encouragement, we learned that while customs may be different in Rwanda, they are not wrong. Only different.

We'll always cherish the days we lived there and the lifelong friendships my family and I made. Even when we transitioned back to the US to pastor a church in Oklahoma City, Oklahoma, our work and relationships in Rwanda continued.

Pastoring a local church was challenging and outside my regular gifting with which I had felt comfortable. It was the first time in my Christian life that I realized that not everyone who calls themselves Christian understands the love that we are to show one another as Christ followers. There were many days when my wife and I would struggle, trying to understand this new assignment God had given us. We worked, prayed, and tried our best to follow the leading of the Holy Spirit to take the necessary steps to grow the church and see others come to a saving knowledge of Jesus. In some regards, we welcomed this new challenge and learning opportunity, but the Rwandan people were never far from our hearts.

Then, in January 2014, we were leading our congregation in a twenty-one-day fast. Each night, we opened the church for two hours, so others could come to pray and seek the Lord's direction for the coming year. Little did we know that it was we who would be receiving an unexpected direction.

I believe it was about the tenth day of the fast when I heard God speak to me that we were going to be transitioning back into a full-time missionary role. If you've read my book, Big: Living Bigger Than You Ever Imagined, you'll know why I kept this to myself. God doesn't speak to everyone at the same time. Katina's journey and my journey to belief and then faith, which had started fifteen years earlier, had been exactly what God planned for us. He had been faithful from our troubled beginning before we were saved . . . to organic, life-changing discipleship in a local church . . . through Bible school and entrepreneurship . . . during our tenure as youth ministers . . . while we grappled with the logistics of a call to full-time mission work . . . and throughout the missionary-appointment process of our fellowship. He had seen us through, and I wanted to process and make sure it was truly of God before I spoke to Katina about it.

A few nights later, as we returned home from prayer, Katina asked me a question: "Are you hearing anything from God during this prayer time?"

A little taken aback, I asked her to tell me what she was hearing first. She went on to let me know that she felt that we were about to step back into full-time mission work. Over the next several weeks, God confirmed this to us in a variety of ways, so we met with the church board and made a transition plan.

On Mother's Day, 2014, Advocates for Africa was born. This was NOT an endeavor that would take our family back to the front lines of Africa; rather, it was one in which God birthed a vision to launch an organization that would make an impact far greater than we could ever make on our own living in Africa—an impact that would last beyond our lifetimes.

Many missionaries and organizations we witnessed when living on the field regarded themselves as the "experts" who were there to get the local people "lined out." Our experience was much different. In fact, we quickly realized that the Rwandan people not only had a great desire to help their own people but also had many of the skills to do so. They only lacked a little structure, training, and the finances to do that at a level of greater impact.

We quickly realized that the Rwandan people not only had a great desire to help their own people but also had many of the skills to do so. They only lacked a little structure, training, and the finances to do that at a level of greater impact.

I remember countless lunches with my Rwandan friends during which one of them would lead the waitress to Christ right there at the table. Other times, they would organize large outreaches where thousands of people would gather to hear the gospel. This led me to believe that our role would be that of an advocate for Africa rather than someone coming with all the answers. We would encourage, equip, train, and help provide structure, strategy, and even finances to see the work move forward.

I quickly realized that if you want to change the world, you have to be able to pay for it. So I began doing what I had learned previously as a frontline traditional, if you will, missionary. Speaking with pastors and asking them for time on a Sunday morning to present our mission quickly became our only model of raising the money we needed to fund the first few ministry endeavors we had.

Pastors were quick to open their pulpits for us. For that, we will always be thankful. God's grace and His gifting on my life as a communicator opened the doors we needed. The first few years were amazing. Our vision was rather small, and my preaching schedule could fund it all. I was excited about this new direction and the fact that we had launched an organization. This passion fueled me as we traveled and spoke to congregations of all sizes. People began to help with funding, and good things were happening.

Then, about three years into this traditional model, God began to expand the vision. Suddenly, we were recognizing needs on the continent of Africa that were well beyond our current ability to fund. Increasing my speaking schedule simply wasn't an option. Quite honestly, I was already feeling a little burnout from the hard push we made just getting the organization off the ground.

Now, I felt the vision expanding, but how were we going to fund these great projects solely through speaking at churches? It simply was not physically or mentally possible. I was frustrated, to say the least.

Then, a thought hit me. *How do others who do not have a speaking gift raise funds for their organizations?* Many organizations raise millions of dollars, yet they don't speak in a single church. How is this possible?

This question sent me on a multi-year journey to find out. I attended training seminars, hired consultants, and read more books than I can even remember. Each book, seminar, and meeting with a consultant would deposit a little more knowledge in me. Soon, I began to realize that if we could add these tools to the primary funding model of public speaking, we might be able to increase our funding in a major way.

As I began to think through this, one aspect was glaring at me. RETENTION. I found that the nonprofit realm was no different than business in that retaining donors or customers was much more beneficial to the organization than always chasing the next new one. In fact, research has concluded that it's five times as costly to find a new donor than it is to retain those you have.[1] Even more alarming is that the new donor you acquired less than six months ago as a result of your substantial marketing

---

1   Michael DeVoll, "Donor Retention: The Ultimate Guide for Nonprofits," *NonProfitEasy*, 5 Apr. 2022, https://nonprofiteasy.com/ultimate-guide-to-donor-retention/#:~:text=It%20costs%20about%20five%20 times,%2C%20and%20possibly%20only%2C%20donation.

investments is now part of the 54 percent who'll stop giving after only one year.[2]

Specifically, according to Fundraising Donor Management:

> *Based on a survey conducted from 2014 to 2015, from the AFP (Association of Fundraising Professionals) 2016 Fundraising Effectiveness Survey Report, the results determined the average donor retention rate is around 46% with an attrition rate of 54%. This percentage reflects a total amount of $8.6 billion in gifts from 8.27 million donors with average gross revenue of $869,000 from the 9,922 participating organizations.[3]*

Now, you might be thinking that this is because people are flaky or inconsistent, but that isn't always the case. When these people were asked why they didn't make a repeat gift, do you know what the number one answer was? "Because no one asked me."

When I read this, it stung because our organization was falling into the same trap. I was so focused on the next speaking engagement or the next fundraiser that I was all but ignoring those who had already supported our mission in the past. To be honest, it wasn't so much that I didn't want to build deeper relationships with them, but I was too exhausted traveling and planning

---

2 Steve Goodman, "Why Your Donor Retention Rate Is Lousy and How to Fix It," Arjuna Solutions, https://www.arjunasolutions.com/blog/why-your-donor-retention-rate-is-lousy-and-how-to-fix-it.

3 Cameron C. Lanphear, "What Is Donor Retention and How Do I Maintain It Year after Year?" Sustainsoftware, 4 Apr. 2017, https://www.sustainsoftware.com/post/2017/03/20/what-is-donor-retention-and-how-do-i-maintain-it-year-after-year.

fundraisers to adequately follow up. Secondly, I had no strategy to remind myself to do so. This is a critical error for nonprofits because if you don't have the ability to grow your network of friends, you probably won't increase your funding.

> **If you don't have the ability to grow your network of friends, you probably won't increase your funding.**

It was during that season that I decided we must make a fundamental shift in our fundraising process if we were truly going to fund all that God had placed in my heart. The old traditional model was wonderful for frontline work alone but would never sustain an organization that wanted to fund multimillion dollar projects and expand into every country in Africa.

The pages that follow outline the exact strategy we began using to raise more money than we would have ever been able to do using our traditional model. In fact, this God-given strategy has helped us shift from raising a backbreaking $50,000-$100,000 each year to raising more than $7 million over the last few years. Keep in mind that this didn't happen with a large development team of experienced fundraising professionals. Up to that point, our organization only had one fundraiser. Me.

If you are just getting started, or maybe you're like me and starting to realize that the funding you need can't be raised using your current system, this book will help. I encourage you to view this for what it is: a strategy to retain more donors and raise more money. A simple illustration that may help as you move forward is to think of a pipeline. In the same way a pipeline directs valuable liquid from one place to another, this strategy evolves friends into donors who will make repeat investments in your cause year after year. And best of all, it will provide you with a simple structure for maintaining meaningful relationships—which equals more funding.

If you're ready to start raising more funding for your cause so you can help those in need, turn the page, and let's get to work.

CHAPTER 1

COMMUNICATION: THE FOUNDATION OF FUNDRAISING

W e rented a small airplane and left Addis Ababa, Ethiopia, before the sun was up. We traveled for about thirty minutes before the sun started to crest over the mountains, revealing the jagged peaks and lush valleys below. We flew for some time before making a few passes over an enormous field that seemed to appear out of nowhere.

As we passed over the field, I could see the pilot checking the makeshift landing strip for obstructions. Children began running from the nearby villages to see the airplane. We took one more pass before the pilot began making the necessary adjustments to land the plane. I was nervous.

Closer, closer, closer . . . touchdown. It was about as soft as you can imagine landing in a field in Africa would be. The moment the plane came to a stop and the engine was powered down, we were greeted by a few dozen children. Some were scared, some were curious, and others wanted to touch our skin to see if we were real.

We were there to conduct a four-day gospel crusade. Each afternoon, I would watch the field swell with people until, by the fourth afternoon, over 275,000 people had gathered. It was overwhelming to see that many people, many of whom I learned had walked for weeks to get there. The roar of the crowd when they got excited about the preaching was deafening. It was surreal to see that many people in one place.

On day three, I walked into a small church where an outreach meal to feed orphaned children was being prepared. As I approached, I could see smoke rising from the window of the kitchen. The smell of the food wafted along with it. The small, simple bush church had mud walls and a tin roof. There were a few Ethiopian women preparing food, and at the back of the church stood a small double door made from bamboo. Through the cracks in the door, I could see dozens of children peeking through the openings in amazement at the first white man they had ever seen.

When the time came, the doors were opened, and I watched the children flood into the church and begin sitting down on the tiny wooden benches they used as pews. The children were wearing rags as clothes, and the overwhelming smell of dirt and body odor filled the small space. None of the children wore shoes. Swollen stomachs and hair loss were evident—all because of malnutrition. At this point in my life, I hadn't witnessed this level of poverty and injustice firsthand.

As we began handing children plates of food, they were elated. Soon sadness was replaced with smiles and laughter, and I have to admit, I felt pretty good about it all up to that point. As most were finishing up their meals, a single boy around the age of five slowly stumbled in through the back door. He was late, completely alone, scared, and hungry.

As he walked closer, I noticed that he had a small piece of rope around his waist to gather the fabric that fell from his shoulders and was serving as his upper garment. He was losing his hair like the other children, had swollen hands and feet, and was tucking a lame hand against his ribcage. He moved closer to me, looking for a plate of food but stopped short as if he became fearful of the man standing before him. I motioned for the Ethiopian ladies to bring another plate of food.

Handing the plate of food to the little boy, he balanced it on top of his hand and found a place to sit on the small wooden benches. Trying to eat while balancing the plate of food proved to be hard for him, so I sat beside him to hold the plate, so he could eat. He dug his good hand into the food but never took his eyes off me. He ate fast, as though the food would be taken from him at some point.

This encounter changed me forever. *Who would feed this child when we left for America?* The question haunted me for the next several days until, finally, on the airplane ride home, I began to argue with God. "Why would you allow this to happen," I remember muttering under my breath. Then, I had an overwhelming sense that God was asking me the same question.

Why would YOU allow this to happen?

That was the day I knew I would spend the rest of my life doing everything in my power to feed, clothe, provide shelter, and educate children in Africa.

That's my story. What is yours?

YOUR STORY

Your story is the most important and powerful tool you have. Most likely, you are reading this because something happened in your life that changed the way you think. You witnessed a wrong in the world, and you felt a strong desire to correct that wrong. You started a nonprofit, you became a missionary, you stepped into ministry, you pastor a church, or you started a business, but it all started with a story. Your story.

> **Your story is the most important and powerful tool you have.**

Regardless of whether you are in ministry or business, stories capture people's attention and pull them into the causes we believe in. Everyone loves a good story! Want to raise more money for your organization? Need to increase sales in your company? Starting a building campaign for your church? A compelling story is where it begins.

A great story is powerful in two ways:

1) It helps people remember your cause.
2) It helps them retell others about your cause.

That's why it's imperative that all leaders become master storytellers!

So, where does that begin?

MOTIVATION

There must be a deep motivation that drives you to pursue your cause. If not, others will sense it, and your vision won't be attractive to them. Answering the following questions will help you focus your story and tell it with the passion that holds people's attention and moves them to action.

- What wrong have you witnessed that you want to correct?
- Why do you care about this issue?
- What makes you angry about this?
- What are you going to do about it?
- Do you have a passion for it?
- Does it keep you up at night?

PRO TIP: *Remind yourself why you started. Write down the answers to all these questions, and review them on days when things are tough.*

THE MESSAGE

The content of your message should be filled with interesting points that someone can engage with. Using greater detail when describing events, places, and situations will result in a more captivated listener.

What are the keys to great storytelling? Writers developed a logical flow of storytelling many years ago. Books and movies have used that outline to deliver some of the most powerful messages in history. By following the same formula, you can be assured of becoming a great storyteller yourself!

Story Elements

Below are the elements of a great story as they relate to my experience in Ethiopia.

Characters—The children who greeted the plane, the Ethiopian volunteers, the orphaned children, and I were the characters mentioned in my story.

Setting—Ethiopia, mountain terrain, mud church, dusty streets.

Plot—This includes the events that took place to bring you to where you are today. For me, it was going to Ethiopia, meeting the little boy, wrestling with the injustice of starving children, and deciding to do something about it.

Conflict—Who would feed these children?

Resolution—God spoke to me to respond.

Help Them Feel It

Following this format, mixing in effective quality adjectives as you explain each portion will help transport your listener to the story, which helps them "feel" what you felt. That is one of your goals. If your listeners don't feel the injustice, they may not be motivated to help. Passion and conviction help accomplish this. Use descriptive words.

Help Them Follow It

The storytelling model works well because it's easy for the listener to gain clarity, understand your cause, and forward it along to others. In order for the listener to have clarity, you must first have it yourself.

Here are a few strategies to get clarity, so you can communicate your message effectively:

- Write it—over and over. Each time you do, you'll remember more details that are important to share.
- Tell it—over and over. Doing this helps you not only get the message out but also provides you with feedback regarding what portions of the story others are most interested in. You'll begin to notice the parts when people really lean in to listen closely.
- Film yourself speaking it—over and over. You'll get a wealth of information from doing this. After filming, watch it with the sound off. What do your nonverbal gestures say? Do

you look angry, sad, or indifferent? Next, listen to the audio with no video. Are you believable? Do you communicate conviction and passion?

So, you've identified your motivation and begun working on the message and its delivery. What logical step do you think could be next?

MARKETING

The greatest cause in the world will go unfunded if no one knows about it. Marketing is simply the delivery of your message to the right audience. This comes in many different formats, but for now, focus on these foundational considerations.

Hiring a Marketing Company

This may be an attractive solution to your marketing needs, and if you can afford it, that's great. But, for most nonprofit start-ups, the budget isn't there yet. What are the basics of marketing you need now? I suggest you ask yourself where your target audience would naturally find you. Then, concentrate your efforts there to begin.

- Website
- Print pieces
- Social media
- Video

Whatever You Do, Do It Very Well

I can't stress this enough. If you only have enough funding to create one great piece of marketing, leave the other aspects of marketing until later. A bad piece of marketing will harm your efforts. This is why it's important to choose the best avenue to start with and do it with excellence. Then, add the other elements later.

PRO TIP: *Use Fiverr, a global online marketplace for freelancers, instead of friends. Friends don't care about deadlines, and you can't fire them. Just because you know someone who _____, doesn't mean they are good at it. Free is rarely good, and good is rarely free.*

These are foundational pieces that must be taken seriously, but they won't fund your cause. You need motivation, a good message told well, and a few marketing materials. But now . . . you need MONEY! How do you get it? How do you keep it? We'll be discussing this and more in the chapters that follow.

CHAPTER 2

IDENTIFICATION: LIVING FUNDRAISER TO FUNDRAISER

I recently worked with an organization that had an incredible mission and made a great impact on children overseas. Their staff was small, but they worked really hard on their fundraisers. In the first few years, they were able to draw some serious donations through these efforts. They naturally used these to build their projects, which soon needed employees, maintenance, grounds crews, and managers. Considering they had a good amount of funding, this didn't seem like a problem.

A few years and building projects later, they realized they didn't have the recurring capital needed to sustain it all. Nor did they have the energy to continue all the fundraising events. This left them in a serious situation because those they are helping and the team they've put together are all counting on them to continue their efforts.

There are many people who can toss you fundraising ideas that can bring funding to your organization. However, if your funding strategy is solely based on these events, you'll soon be exhausted—mentally and physically. Moreover, you will build an organization that you won't be able to sustain. Talk about stress!

> **If your funding strategy is solely based on fundraising events, you'll soon be exhausted—mentally and physically.**

A LESS STRESSFUL MODEL

Once you realize that your multitude of fundraising events is exhausting you and not raising the funding you need, it's time to consider another way.

Consider the following:

- It costs ten times more to acquire a new donor than it does to keep one.[4]
- Over half of your donors who give a one-time gift will NOT MAKE A SECOND GIFT—EVER! [5]
- When polled as to why, the number one answer was, "No one asked me!" [6]
- A donor or customer who has given twice before is 60 percent more likely to donate again! [7]

4 Ali Oligny and Shammy Peterson, "Asking Your Donors to Give Again," The Modern Nonprofit, 1 Nov. 2021, https://themodernnonprofit.com/asking-your-donors-to-give-again/.

5 Steve Goodman, "Why Your Donor Retention Rate Is Lousy and How to Fix It."

6 Tina Jepson, "Donor Retention: Why Donors Don't Give Second Gifts" CauseVox, 7 Oct. 2020, https://www.causevox.com/blog/why-donors-dont-give-second-gifts/.

7 Arslan Javaid, "How to Get a 2nd Gift from New Donors," The Fundraising Authority, 19 May 2018, https://thefundraisingauthority.com/donor-cultivation/new-donors-second-gift/#:~:text=However%2C%20once%20a%20new%20donor,will%20make%20a%20third%20gift.

Those numbers are staggering! Think about that: ten times more, over half, and 60 percent! This is a very simple point, but it is worth mentioning at the beginning of this discussion. Do not, under any circumstances, forget to ask your donors for a gift during your next campaign. It is key!

So, let me ask you: Would it change your budget if you could retain even 10 percent of those? What about 20 percent? Or even 50 percent? Imagine keeping these percentages of donors while continuing to add new ones each year! Do you see how this begins to create exponential growth? Add to that the fact that retained donors recruit new donors.[8]

Sadly, businesses and nonprofits alike spend most of their time and MONEY gaining new donors or customers when experts agree that it's five times more costly to gain a new relationship than cultivate the ones you have.

How do we get caught in this trap?

First, you may be spending so much time organizing your fund-raising events that you don't have any time to connect with your existing donor base. Secondly, as your organization grows, demands on your time will make it difficult to adequately cultivate existing relationships as well.

---

8 Jay Love, "Donor Retention Math Made Simple." Bloomerang, 10 May 2022, https://bloomerang.co/blog/donor-retention-math-made-simple/.

This becomes problematic for two reasons. First, those who joined your cause early and had personal contact with you often will continue to want the same. With two hundred donors this is possible, but with one thousand donors, not so much.

Secondly, when donors don't feel personally connected, donor attrition becomes staggering. Simply said, you might be bringing more funding in the front door through your fundraising events, but you'll be losing funding out the back door in droves. This may not seem like a huge issue at first, but in the long run, you'll be creating a system that has to be fed continuously to stay alive.

This is why RETENTION is the fastest and most beneficial way to grow your organizational funding over the long haul. However, in order to retain more donors, you need a strategy in place to manage more relationships than you currently are able to. Think of it like a pipeline.

Your job now becomes funneling potential new donors or customers into your pipeline, so you can move them from acquaintances to lifelong donors! This means there must be traffic coming into the pipeline, and the pipeline must keep that traffic moving in order to operate.

I'm *not* suggesting that funding that is derived from fundraisers isn't important. I'm also *not* suggesting that you remove them from your yearly funding plan altogether; you may need to cut back, though, on the number of these events you're currently having. What I *am* suggesting is that you need a different mindset for the goal of these types of events.

In this strategy, how you handle the donors that are involved in such events is even more important than the events themselves. So let's dive in and start building a funding model that can provide sustainable growth!

Let's take a look at the first step: Identification.

IDENTIFICATION

Where do new donors come from? To answer this question, it seems logical to ask where your current donors came from. I would venture to say that your first few donors were, in large part, comprised of your close friends and family. Most nonprofits begin with a vision to help someone in need; then, as they begin putting structure to their vision, they communicate it to friends and family who want to help.

Donating is a trust issue for many. People want to help those in need but don't trust their money will be used appropriately.

Research overwhelmingly suggests that people support the causes their friends are involved in. It's a trust issue for many. People want to help those in need but don't trust their money will be used appropriately. However, when they have a friend who works for the organization, they jump on board and want to help at a deeper level.

Knowing this, it stands to reason that you don't need more donors. You need more friends! But, if you're like most people, you don't have a strategy to find more friends, so your friend base is naturally small. The friendships you have now are with people you attended school with, work with, live next door to, or worship with. They happened organically. This is the natural way to find friends. But, if you want to fully fund your vision, you need a strategy to find additional friends.

Not all of these new friends will be part of your inner circle, but I have found that as I work to build more friendships, every once in a while, I develop a friendship with someone who becomes more like family. This new family member normally becomes a champion for my cause. They become passionate about what we are doing and begin sharing our work with an entirely new network of people. And it all started by putting in the work to find new friends.

Any organization that wants to increase its impact must be able to identify new potential donors or customers to be successful. Why do some excel at this while others struggle? To find out, let's cover some basics of the identification process.

There are two parts to identifying new donors:

1) Networking
2) Acquisition models

Networking

I'll begin with the first because the ability of a fundraiser to network will determine their level of success in all other aspects. Learning to network effectively is similar to studying a fighting style such as Brazilian jujitsu. As with any fighting style, it's lifelong study that makes you a master. However, beginning with the basics is the only place to start down this path.

These five fundamentals of networking will get you started.

1) **Talk to everyone.** I once started a conversation with a gentleman and his wife in an airport. We spoke for roughly fifteen minutes. Two weeks later, he sent me a check for $50,000. You never know whom you're sitting next to on a plane or standing in line with. Talking to everyone also helps you learn the art of good conversation.

2) **Be interested in people.** Don't talk about your mission too quickly and maybe not at all at first meeting someone. Instead, ask them questions about their family, work, hobbies, reasons for traveling, etc. People love talking about themselves and usually feel interested in people who are interested in them. In fifteen minutes, I learned that the couple in the airport was traveling the world, and he was a

retired doctor. I would have never learned that if I was just trying to work in the fact that I was doing mission work.

3) **Be patient.** Every intelligent person can notice when someone is rushing the conversation to talk about themselves or bypassing the relationship just to make an "ask." Have you ever had a conversation with someone you could tell was just waiting for you to finish, so they could talk again? If they aren't a self-centered person (and some are, but do you want to associate too much with that sort of person?), the conversation will eventually come back to YOUR LIFE and the things you're passionate about.

4) **Add VALUE.** Don't stand at the conference exit with your business cards in your hand. I've actually seen people do this! This screams, "I'm desperate!" and people will avoid desperate. Relax, be cool, and don't be quick to tell people what you do. As mentioned, be interested in others. Ask about their work, family, and desires. LISTEN for areas where you can add value to someone else.

A while back, I met a pastor at a conference who I knew was leading a large church. I was introduced to him by one of my board members. There were several pastors standing there engaged in conversation, so I just listened quietly. The conversation topic was burnout in ministry, and the pastor mentioned that he did his PhD work on the subject. When there was a natural pause in the conversation, I simply said, "Pastor, tell me more about the study you've done on this subject. I'm meeting so many ministers leaving the ministry, and I would love to be able to help them." It's a genuine concern of mine.

For the next fifteen minutes, he told me the things he learned during the study. It was true ministry gold that could help so many people! I promptly asked him if he would mind sending me a copy of his dissertation and if I could share his work with people who might benefit. He agreed, and by the time the next conference session was over, he had emailed me his work. After reviewing the work, I asked him if he'd ever considered publishing it for a wider audience, and he said he had thought about it. I was then able to connect him with a friend that helps ministers do just that.

Few things can build a friendship quicker than providing a contact or resource that helps them move forward. But, there are other benefits of networking this way which brings me to the last fundamental.

5) **Collect and catalog contacts.** Taking from the example above, suppose you say, "Hey, I have a friend you need to meet. I think he can help you in this. Can I text you his contact info?" Now, you have their cell number and can stay in touch. A few days later, you may have an additional resource that might help, but you're going to need to email them. You simply send a text like, "I enjoyed our chat the other day. I was thinking about your situation today, and I may have found a pdf (or something similar) that you need to see. Shoot me your email, and I'll send it right over." Now you have a number and email.

   Then, catalog those names like your mission depends on it— because it does! Funding your mission is impossible if you don't have a collection of contacts that may be interested in your work. These contacts need to be collected and cataloged in a way you can recall them. These collected names are vital because you'll funnel them into your donor pipeline.

> ## If your network isn't growing, your bank statement will soon be showing!

If your network isn't growing, your bank statement will soon be showing! There are multiple resources to help you create a database of names. For now, you might consider using Excel. Just remember that you'll want a system that allows you to recall and review the following information before you contact any of them:

- Who they are—Make a bio of what you know. Married to Jill, 3 children (one in college), loves golf, working on a PhD, etc.
- What they do—Attorney, large/med/small church pastor, business owner—coffee shop, etc.
- Contact info—Cell/email/work number, etc.
- Notes—Record and date all interactions you have with the person. Each contact should be a continuation of the last conversation.

As your organization grows, you'll want the ability to classify names according to specific categories. For example: major donor, type of donor (church, business, individual), location, and even types of gifts from the past. This becomes important as you begin to target donors more specifically to where they like to give. Or imagine you want to do a small dinner in their area. You'll need to quickly pull up a list of your relationships in that geographical area to send the invites.

These advanced features can be found in most of the donor software I discovered from a quick Google search for resources. If you decide to jump into a good donor management system right away, do yourself a favor, and find one that has an entry-level product. That way, you can bump up to the next-level product as your organization grows. My personal favorite for this is Blackbaud. They have an incredible number of products that serve both small and large organizations.

PRO TIP: *Download the 2Do app, and create a folder called "Catch Bin." Each time you meet someone new, make a quick note about what you know. It will be an easy way to record their info and a reminder to add them to your donor pipeline. I use this all the time at conferences when I'm meeting many people in a short amount of time.*

You might be thinking, *What if my existing network is small?* That's okay for now, but you'll need to change that if you plan to fund your cause.

The MILLION DOLLAR METHOD

You can start tackling this issue right away in two ways:

1) **Start where you are.** Realize that you already have some relationships; they may just be on life support. Make a list of every person you know—literally everyone who comes to mind. Save the list in a separate Excel document or something similar, and keep it handy. Let's call this your "Leads" list. Think of the places you go and the people you interact with on a monthly basis. The gym, church, work, family, customers, friends, or school activities. Start building a list of the people you meet at these places. Not just friends, but EVERYONE you know. Add names to the list as they come to mind over the next several weeks. We'll come back to this list during the cultivation process.

2) **Identify new places you can make more friends, and get involved.** You can use your leads list from above with a separate row called "Places." Remember that people like helping worthy causes, but they LOVE helping their friends who have worthy causes. Think networks of people: civic clubs, denominational meetings, business groups, school committees, etc. Get out, and get involved somewhere. If you're not willing to meet new people, you're likely not going to raise much money.

Now that you're on your way to being a master networker, let's turn our attention to the next aspect of identifying new donors.

Acquisition Models

An acquisition model is simply *how* you plan to acquire or identify potential new donors. These models act as the net that is cast to pull in potential new relationships. Just as a fisherman must know where to cast his net, you, too, must know where your potential donors are and the best way to make your presentation.

When it comes to donor acquisition, you will have a core model and various submodels. Your core model is natural for you. It's a consistent way of identifying potential new donors or receiving funding. Submodels are supplemental and sometimes experimental. How you identify these models will take some work, and they are generally different for each organization. It's important to understand that there will be some trial and error when it comes to choosing what works best for you.

As you work through this process, keep a few things in mind:

- Capacity (staff/volunteer size and capabilities)—It can be fun to put on a large event, but do you have the organizational capability it takes for a large event? This isn't to say you can't do a large event with many moving parts, but you might consider the frequency of such events. Even putting on an annual gala can be possible but very daunting.
- R.O.I. (Return on Investment)—Estimate how much funding you expect; then divide that by the number of hours you estimate it will take to plan and execute the project. As you try various acquisition models, you'll quickly figure out which ones bring the biggest return. Remember: return

can be the number of names you were able to collect and/ or funding. There is nothing wrong with designing an event for the sole purpose of capturing new contacts to cultivate.

- Sustainability—Can you keep this going? If the answer is a clear no, but you've found the ROI to be worth it, this is most generally a submodel that can be done once per year.

I want to state again that this is an area that is difficult for someone else to define for you because it is very specific to your natural gifting, existing network, current resources, urgency of the funding need, and yearly budget you need to cover. Below are just a few acquisition models that I've found to be effective over the years.

> **Your acquisition model is an area that is difficult for someone else to define for you because it is very specific to your natural gifting, existing network, current resources, urgency of the funding need, and yearly budget you need to cover.**

Here are a few models that I've seen work.

Public Speaking—I begin with this one because it has been my core model for many years. If you are or can learn to be a gifted speaker, it will open many doors for you to share your passion for the cause. Churches, small groups, Sunday schools, men's/women's meetings, and even community clubs are all great avenues for this. Remember: as with all acquisition meetings, you'll be sure to have contact cards available and even registration to collect names. NEVER FORGET that you need the contact names to feed into your pipeline! Always feed the pipeline!

Hosted Dinner Events—These are great when first starting out. They provide a way for those who already believe in your cause to become a champion to their friends by hosting a dinner party at their house or office. They invite a few friends and provide dinner, and you give a presentation of your work. I love this model for many nonprofits because each time you get a champion, you can ask them to host a dinner. It's repeatable, and your champion does most of the work for you. When considering who can champion your cause, think of those who might already have a network of influence. Many times, these small dinners can be underwritten by a special donor who really believes in you, resulting in no expense for your organization.

Open Houses—If you have a physical place to which you can bring people to show them the work you do, this can be a viable model. Nothing is more impactful than showing potential donors the work firsthand. Any excuse to get people "on the ground" with your cause is worth it!

Fundraising Events—We're talking about donor acquisition here, but don't discount your regular events like annual galas or golf tournaments. These can be used to identify potential new donors. At a gala, for example, you can encourage those already involved to bring a friend who they think may be interested. This can be done through an email where you provide a sample email with a registration link that they can simply copy and paste into an email to send to their friends. The same can be done for social media posts.

If you're not feeding the pipeline, your organization will eventually plateau.

Each of the tools mentioned here is for one purpose: adding names to your identification list. Each new relationship you form must be added to this list—regardless of whether it comes from a personal interaction or an event you hosted. Remember: if you're not feeding the pipeline, your organization will eventually plateau.

CHAPTER 3

QUALIFICATION: DOING YOUR HOMEWORK

W e've all had moments when we were embarrassed. They're not enjoyable. The only thing worse than being embarrassed is being the cause of embarrassment to those you care about. Most people wouldn't do it intentionally, yet many fundraising professionals unknowingly do this to donors.

WHAT JUST HAPPENED?

Imagine this scenario: You've been cultivating the relationship with Frank, a new potential donor, and the time comes to make that ask for funds. You prepare a presentation, or you invite him to lunch with materials in hand about the project you would like him to help fund. The lunch goes great, so you pull out the presentation and begin. You feel like everything is going fantastic. In your heart, you feel that Frank is about to fund $20,000 worth of your project, so you finally get to the moment where you ask, "Frank, would you consider helping us fund this need with a gift of $20,000?"

Frank, with tears in his eyes, looks across the table at you and says one of the following:

"I would love to help, but that's what I make in a year."

"I retired last month."

"I'm not sure if you saw my recent Facebook post. I asked for prayer because I lost my job."

What just happened?

You embarrassed yourself, and even worse, you embarrassed Frank! Now, Frank goes away feeling like what he has to invest in your cause won't make a difference. The feeling you just created in Frank is one of the leading reasons why donors don't make a gift or stop giving altogether. Living with the knowledge that you blew the ask and embarrassed your friend Frank is a hard pill to swallow. Especially when it all was avoidable.

Doing your homework to understand what level of gift Frank might have the capacity to provide is extremely important. Avoiding this step can cause harm and even set the relationship back to a place that might not be recoverable. One of the hardest things to do in fundraising is recover a lost donor, especially when they were embarrassed. This scenario causes donors to look elsewhere for a cause they believe really can use what they have to give.

And there is another reason this is important.

OVER- AND UNDER-ASKING

Let's suppose Frank is a new relationship in your life. You've been connecting often and have even spent a few lunches together. Each time you meet, he is wearing faded jeans and an old ball cap. You've even noticed that Frank is driving a ten-year-old truck with a few dings and scratches. You're excited that your new friend asks lots of questions about your work and realize he is ready for an opportunity to make a gift.

All outward appearances make it seem that Frank is a middle-income earner, so you prepare a casual presentation over coffee where you plan to ask him for a very conservative donation. You find a quiet place to connect with him free of distractions and begin walking him through all the reasons that a gift now would make a big impact.

In reality, the project you are presenting needs $50,000 to put you where you need to be in your fundraising goals, but because Frank drives an older truck and wears faded jeans, you decide to make the ask of $500. You finish your presentation, being careful to stop periodically to ask if he has any questions. As you finish, you look Frank right in the eye and ask, "Frank, would you consider helping with a gift of $500?"

With no hesitation at all, Frank declares, "Absolutely!"

Driving home from the meeting, you call your closest friend, who asks, "How did your meeting go with Frank?"

You tell him about the gift but don't receive the response you expected.

He just responds, "Wow, that's shockingly low for him."

Confused, you ask your friend to explain. He goes on to tell you that Frank is one of the largest oil tycoons in the state and usually gives thousands of dollars each year to causes just like yours. Oops!

Doing a little homework right at the beginning of each new relationship helps you avoid the embarrassment of over-asking and the heartbreak of under-asking.

PRO TIP: *Asking "oil tycoon" Frank for $500 on his first gift might be appropriate in some cases—if you've done your homework, and you're just trying to get Frank on board. I like to call this a starter gift. Many major donors like to start their giving with a small amount just to see how you handle their gift. In fact, I've had multimillionaires make an unsolicited gift of $50-$100 just to test the waters of our organization. Such donors watch to see how quickly they get a response or if you respond at all, if you follow through on the project, and if you adequately follow up after the project is complete.*

Understanding the importance of qualifying each relationship was a GAME CHANGER for our organization. Suddenly, we were developing our associations in a much more careful way because we knew a little more about the individuals. It also helped us know what events specific donors might enjoy based on their interests.

> **Doing a little homework right at the beginning of each new relationship helps you avoid the embarrassment of over-asking and the heartbreak of under-asking.**

This is a vital step because the relationship with a CEO of a large company will be developed in a completely different way than a high school teacher. Everyone has different likes, communication styles, passions for charitable work, and even financial capacity.

So, how do we do the homework and avoid the mistakes mentioned above? Below are four ways you can qualify a new relationship.

1) **Listen for clues.** Each time you speak with Frank, listen for indicators that tell you what giving capacity he may have. Did Frank mention where he works? (You asked because you're becoming a master networker!) Look up his business website. Is he an employee or an owner? Did he give other clues? "We were at our lake home last weekend. . . ." "We just got back from vacation in Italy. . . ." "We have two kids in college—one at Stanford, the other at Yale."

2) **Check out social media.** People will show you their entire lives on social media. This can be another way to determine if Frank takes his family on expensive vacations, drives a luxurious car, lives in an extraordinarily large or small home, or supports other charitable causes. It'll even indicate where he works. In addition, social media can help you discover what Frank is passionate about. Do you have mutual friends that you could reach out to in order to learn more about him? You can learn a lot through social media posts and photos. If appropriate, send him a friend request.

3) **Search public records.** Did you know there are services that will do a wealth check on Frank for you? You don't need his permission, and you don't need much info on Frank to make this happen. These companies use information such as tax filings, property owned, and other public records to give you an idea of Frank's net worth. This can prove to be invaluable for you in determining how to communicate and develop your relationship.

Here are just a few of the companies that provide this for you:

■ www.Iwave.com
■ www.donorsearch.net
■ https://npoinfo.com
■ https://www.givingdna.com
■ https://www.giveffect.com

PRO TIP: *Look for a donor management solution that not only offers donor management but also has a wealth screening service built in.*

---

4) **Google maps.** Use Google maps to take a quick peek at his house if you know the address. Don't know his address? See step 3 above.

> *Insight: The quickest ways to get a general idea of someone's capacity are their occupation and the age, size, and location of their home.*

These qualifying steps may feel creepy to you at first. If you feel this way, consider a paradigm shift. You are a professional relationship builder and fundraiser. It makes sense for a professional to use every tool available to them in order to do the best they can to fund their cause. Those you serve through your cause will be the ones who benefit the most.

Getting an understanding of who your potential donor is helps you develop the relationship with grace and design a gift proposal that's appropriate for their capacity and passion. This will help them feel honored to help and give you the joy of knowing you are helping your cause in the best way.

Donors like to be treated differently depending on what level they are. The funding presentation and how you handle a millionaire business owner is vastly different from that of a blue-collar factory worker. One may want the high-level details, while the other may just want to know the name of the child in your program that their $100 will be helping. Both individuals are equally important to your cause, and qualifying them as early as possible will help you gain both as friends and donors!

RECAP AND PRACTICAL STEPS

Begin making an "A, B, C" list. This list is comprised of everyone you know. These names can be listed in an Excel document with the tab labeled "Identification" because they are people you've identified as potential donors. Remember to list important information about each person next to their name, along with a rating of A, B, or C.

- A's are people like family. They are very likely to support your cause.
- B's are those who, with a little warming up of the relationship, you could expect to become donors.
- C's are those who will need much more cultivation in order to become donors.

Each week, you'll be adding names to the identification list. At the same time, your mission shifts to moving a few names to a new tab on the same spreadsheet, but call this one "Qualification." Simply cut and paste the entire row of data from the identification list to the qualification list as you schedule time to do your research. Essentially, you are moving them from one list to the other in small batches.

Follow the steps listed above to research each potential donor on the qualification list. Be sure to add the information you are learning while doing your homework on each person. Data such as home size, occupation, family situation, age, and even potential capacity level should be added.

PRO TIP: *Deciding what your organization considers a modest, intermediate, or major gift will help you categorize the new relationships on your qualification list. Simply mark each person's data with what level they might be. As you get to know your potential donor better, you can adjust this before making an ask for funding.*

Feeding your donor pipeline (identification) and doing your research (qualification) should now become a scheduled part of your week as a fundraising professional. Making this a priority will help you approach new relationships in a more strategic way and prepare you for the next step of the process. Step 3 is Cultivation. We'll take a look at it next.

CHAPTER 4

CULTIVATION: THE ART OF "FRIEND" RAISING

WHERE WOULD WE BE WITHOUT FARMERS?

''ve had the opportunity to travel all over the US for speaking engagements. I try to fly to these engagements as often as possible. There is something calming to me about flying. Maybe it's the fact that I can turn off my phone, don't have a meeting to attend, or can just enjoy a few hours of writing with few interruptions. I'm not exactly sure why, but I've always enjoyed flying. Everything looks different from thirty thousand feet. A view from the window always reveals the vast amount of land that stretches from coast to coast.

Much of this land is used for farming. For hundreds of miles, blankets of farmland produce crops such as wheat, soybeans, and corn. This precious produce is vital to the survival of those living in the US. I thank God for the hard-working farmers who feed our nation. It's humbling to think of how many hours these farmers put in to produce a single crop.

YOU ARE IMPORTANT TO THOSE IN NEED

These farmers are much like nonprofit leaders. Without farmers growing the produce we need, people would suffer; without the work of nonprofit leaders like you, those you're called to serve will likely do the same. That's why leaving your vision unfunded simply isn't an option. Consider how important this makes you! You may be the only link between someone's suffering and their breakthrough. Like the farmer, you have a cause that will help people, so it's imperative that you cultivate the ground of your relationships to help produce the crop you need.

IT'S TIME TO SHIFT OUR THINKING

I attend an incredible church. Each week, I worship with former gang members, bikers, bankers, suburban families, single parents, and businesspeople. One of those business people comes from a family that ranks in the top one hundred wealthiest in the world. He, along with many other high-net-worth individuals, has helped shift my thinking concerning the role of a nonprofit leader and fundraiser.

One gentleman said to me, "Jerod, I'm good at making money and creating jobs that provide for families. What I'm not so good at is knowing where my charitable dollars should go or whom I can trust with handling those dollars in a responsible way. That's why guys like me need guys like you."

YOU ARE IMPORTANT TO THOSE WHO WANT TO HELP

Every farmer nurtures a seed that must go through the process of germination. Careful attention is given to protect the seed and give it every possibility to grow into something that is useful to others. The process is quite remarkable when you pause to consider everything that must align for this to happen.

First, the seed must "wake up." This doesn't happen just because the soil conditions are right. In fact, a seed will only begin to germinate when it's placed in an environment where temperature, moisture, oxygen, and the correct light conditions are present. Subtract any of these conditions, and the seed will lie dormant forever. To make it even more interesting, different seeds require a different ratio of each condition. That's why the farmer must be well-educated about each seed.

> I believe people have a built-in desire to help the world be a better place to live; they've just never been in the right environment to act on it.

The relationships you have now are much the same. I believe people have a built-in desire to help the world be a better place to live; they've just never been in the right environment to act on it. That's where you come in. Your job is to create the right conditions for your friends to produce something of value to others. Simply put, when you cultivate your relationships in this way, they "wake up" to all the good they can do by helping your cause. This isn't just to produce funding for your work; it's to help your friends realize how much they have to offer those in need. After all, would a good friend do anything less?

Your job as a professional nonprofit leader is to act as the farmer who wants to create the right conditions for individuals, businesses, and even governments to explore their philanthropic interests. In this way, you act more like a guide who helps others help the world. You're cultivating a channel they can trust, so they feel good about supporting a cause that is worthy. This doesn't happen by accident. It takes work, intentionality, and forethought. It takes cultivation.

FRIENDSHIP FIRST—ALWAYS

Let's continue with our example of Frank from our previous talks. Let's say you met Frank at a conference, and you found a way to stay in touch. You placed him on your identification list and even did a great job of qualifying him, so you know what level of donor he might be. Is he now ready for an ask? NO WAY!

PRO TIP: *Cultivate the friendship—not the donation. Bypassing the relationship factor of fundraising is like a farmer digging up the seed he just planted or, worse yet, digging up the seed at the first signs of sprouting. This can damage your relationship and forfeit any chance you have to make a lifelong friend and donor. Build lifelong friendships, and you'll build lifelong donors.*

But I need money now! you may be thinking. I get it; really, I do. Funding demands never go away, and the moment you get one project funded, another seems to take its place. But have you stopped to consider that the reason you may be in this pressure situation is because you predominantly go straight for the donation and not the friendship? Could you be moving things along so quickly that Frank begins to notice that you are only interested in his money and not his life?

EVERY RELATIONSHIP HAS A PACE

Do you remember your dating experiences in the past? When we are dating someone, we do everything possible to get to know the person. We go to dinner, talk on the phone for hours, and even drive hundreds of miles just to be with them. We didn't mind doing any of that because we were cultivating a relationship that we wanted to last a long time. However, do you also remember the relationships that seemed to be moving too fast? They created anxiety for you and the other person and cheapened the entire relationship process. That's the same feeling someone receives if you try to bypass the relationship and go straight for the donation.

Think about it. Frank probably doesn't know enough about your organization to even make an educated contribution. Do you know what Frank is passionate about, how many children he has, how long he has been married, or where he was raised as a child? Does Frank consider you a friend or just an acquaintance? Why would someone want to make a sizable donation to your cause when they don't really know you, and you've not made a genuine effort to get to know them? This isn't far from standing on a street corner asking total strangers for a gift to support your cause. Sure, you'll get a few that feel sorry for you and drop some change in the bucket, but they won't ever become lifelong donors that support your work year after year. It doesn't feel right for you or for them.

I'll say it again. Friendship first—Always.

Now that we've established the motivation for intentionally cultivating friendships let's talk about what it takes to build these kinds of long-term relationships.

I'll say it again. Friendship first—Always.

Begin by thinking about the closest friends you have. You probably didn't meet these people and become instant BFFs. (That's a term we use in the US that stands for "Best Friends Forever.") It took time for you to realize that your friend was someone you could trust and be vulnerable with. Over time, a relationship formed, and you gained a friend.

Think about your friend and what qualities they have that make them good friendship material. What was it about this person that caused you to consider spending more time with them? If you don't have a few great friends to think this out, make a list of qualities that you would expect from a really great friend. Realize that the qualities that make a great friend are universal. What you would look for in a friend are the same qualities that others look for in their friendships as well. If you want to grow your network of friends, you'll need to daily display these traits to those around you.

So, what does it take to be a great friend? I believe the following four keys will help you cultivate deeper, longer-lasting friendships that will bring you lifelong donors.

Be Friendly

This sounds simple, but you wouldn't believe how many people don't understand basic manners. Saying, "Yes, please," or "No, thank you," have all but been forgotten in our world. Basic rules of culture, like holding the door open for the person behind you and saying, "Thank you," when someone does it for you, are quickly slipping away. All you need to do is enter a local restaurant, and you'll quickly find that being courteous is a lost art. The good news about this is that it won't take much to stand out to those around you if you're willing to just . . . well . . . be friendly!

If you were not raised in a home where this was expected, it may not come naturally for you. If this is true of your situation, pick up some resources that can help you learn exceptional customer service. Many of the resources of this nature are nothing more than basic courtesy.

PRO TIP: *Create a custom card with your name embossed on it—not your organization name—your name. (Friendship first. Always). Place a stack of them on your desk for easy access and to remind yourself to say thank you often. Send them to anyone you want to appreciate. This not only shows you to be friendly, but it also helps to keep you on the radar of the recipient.*

Practice Active Listening

Active listening is your verbal and nonverbal cues to the speaker that you're staying on track with the conversation. Have you ever had a conversation in which you knew the other person wasn't paying attention? How did that make you feel? This is a tough one for people who may be challenged with attention disorders, so it takes discipline—especially in environments where there are many people and lots of movement.

Here's something I learned from late pastor Billy Joe Daugherty of Victory Church in Tulsa, Oklahoma. He once told me, "The most important person in the world is the one that's standing in front of you at that moment." Practice looking others in the eye, nodding your head, raising your eyebrows, and saying even the occasional "Hmm" to let others know you're interested in what they have to say.

Give Gifts
Even if this isn't their love language, everyone enjoys receiving the occasional gift. It will give them a pleasant surprise and a reason to think well of you. Do your homework to find something that would genuinely be of interest to them.

When meeting businesspeople or pastors, I've called back a few days after the meeting to speak with their assistant. These amazing people can tell you their favorite sports team, restaurants they like to frequent, places they like to shop, and a host of other information. A simple gift card to one of these places, a sleeve of their favorite golf balls, or even tickets to an event they love can create an open door for you to spend more time with this person in the future.

Caution: Never—and I mean NEVER—ignore someone's assistant. That person can be a strong influence in your access to those you're trying to develop a friendship with. These incredible people act as gatekeepers, and if you ever want the gate to be open, they need to love you!

Time

This can't be bypassed! Just as it takes time once a seed has been exposed to the right conditions to grow into a crop, it takes time to build a friendship. So, look for opportunities to be with them. Invite them to a sporting event, another activity that you've learned they like, or even dinner at your house. Any opportunity to be with them, so you can learn more about who they are, will help cultivate the friendship you're looking for. A word of caution here: Don't be creepy. Be patiently persistent instead. You probably don't want to invite someone you met only yesterday on your family vacation. I know that sounds extreme, but I think you get my point here.

Cultivation is the life of the Million Dollar Method process. Disregard the importance of this, and you'll eliminate your ability to raise the funds you need!

CHAPTER 5

ACTIVATION: YOUR PROTECTION AGAINST BECOMING "THAT" FRIEND

My wife, Katina, and I once lived next door to a couple that we enjoyed spending time with when we first met them. Our relationship with this couple began casually, with the occasional conversation across the driveway or at the community pool. As time passed, we began to invite them for dinner because we enjoyed their company, and we had many things in common with them.

After some time, though, we realized that we had never been to their house for dinner. This wasn't too alarming but rather a passing conversation between us a few times. We understand that some people don't like to cook, and some simply don't enjoy hosting others in their homes. Busy schedules can also hinder others from returning the favor of hosting as well. However, as the years went by, it became obvious that something completely different was going on.

It began with our neighbor's wife borrowing a pair of shoes from Katina. Women do this from time to time. No big deal, right? Katina is the kind of person who goes all in with her friendships, so if a friend needs something, she'll gladly help out. But soon, she was getting frustrated about the one-sided wardrobe transactions because each time Katina would ask to borrow something from the neighbor, she was turned down with a host of really bad excuses.

Katina had noticed these items in the neighbor's closet during times her friend needed some outfit advice before an event, yet the neighbor was now saying she didn't own them. The neighbor loved borrowing from Katina, but she didn't like lending items to her in return. You can imagine how irksome it would be to be turned down when asking to borrow something from a friend when you had given them unhindered access to your entire wardrobe, and you know they owned the item you needed.

That wasn't the only irritation. Getting the borrowed items back from the neighbor was also a challenge. It frustrated my wife that she was quick to lend a pair of shoes but then had to chase down our neighbor to get them back. This happened often, and my wife continued to lend her wardrobe whenever her friend needed it, even though each time, my wife would have to go out of her way to retrieve the item. Shoes, scarves, pants, and even accessories such as jewelry were all lent when our friend needed them, and every time, it was a chore to get them back.

Then it dawned on us that the only time this couple actually reached out was when they needed something. There would be long stretches of time where we would reach out to them with no response, yet when it was time to borrow something from us, they were quick to reach out to us. It didn't take long to realize we were being used for what we had instead of loved for who we were. This kind of one-sided friendship will never last long. Why? Because a friendship that isn't reciprocal isn't a friendship. It's a transaction.

AVOID BEING "THAT" FRIEND

Do you know someone like this? Have you ever had "that friend" who only calls you when they need something? You know the ones. You don't hear from the person for a long time; then your phone rings, and as soon as you see the number, you KNOW they are calling to ask you for a favor.

Everyone has encountered that friend, and sadly, some people *are* that friend.

Calling someone only when you need something turns people off—quickly.

> ### Calling someone only when you need something turns people off—quickly.

This is especially true when it comes to fundraising. Remember that people love to support their friends who have great causes, but if you get into the habit of only calling when there is an ask to be made, you'll be breaking the cardinal rule of fundraising.

PLACING MORE PRIORITY ON THE FUNDING THAN THE FRIENDSHIP

As mentioned in the last lesson, get into the habit of putting the funding over the friendship, and you'll soon be having budget problems. The highest calling of a fundraising professional is to connect their friends to the cause they love. It's hard to do that if you aren't making or keeping friends.

That's why the next step in our process is so important.

ACTIVATION

Activating a donor is the process of warming up the relationship before you make an appeal for funds. This is where you will bring your donor intentionally close. You're turning up the vision-casting, talking about what you are doing in your mission, asking them to pray for some pressing needs you have, or informing him of wins you just experienced. The intent here is to remind your friend why they became your friend, but it's also to place your mission square in the middle of their radar. It is NOT to make an appeal for funds.

This step is extremely important for three reasons.

1) Let's suppose you've done a great job of cultivating Frank, and he has truly become a friend. Two years ago, he gave a great donation; then, last year, he did the same. Here it is— year three—and you realize it's been eleven months since Frank's last gift, but you haven't spoken to him since. Oops!

How inappropriate would it be to call Frank after a long stretch of time and ask for a donation? Depending on how long you've known Frank, you could offend him with such an ask and lose him as a friend and a donor forever.

2) As a fundraising professional, you'll be looking at your renewal list monthly. This is the list of donors who made a gift last year but haven't done so this year. Obviously, your goal is to renew them before they lapse on the thirteenth month. Each of us can be guilty of letting a donor fall through the cracks of the cultivation process; then, we are in an awkward position when it comes time to renew them. When we realize this has happened, it simply isn't professional to call them for a donation after a year of no personal contact.

3) Paying attention to your activation list helps you be a good friend on purpose. We all get busy and forget from time to time. Monitoring this list often gives a strategic way for you to maintain good relationships. You may be thinking, But I do a good job of this already, and that may be the truth. However, how well will you do when you have one hundred, two hundred, or even more than three hundred donors to stay in touch with? As your organization grows, you'll have to put a strategy like this in place, so your friendships don't grow cold.

Some reading this may be thinking that at the point your number of donors increases above a specific quantity, they will just hire another fundraising professional to help. This would be amazing in a perfect world. My experience has been that most nonprofits don't have the money to do this. Mission-critical items get funded first, and soon, the founder has a portfolio to handle that simply can't be maintained without a strong system to remind them to connect with each donor.

I would also add here that this is exactly the rationale I used to raise over $7M for the organization I lead. I don't say that to boast but rather to show you that it's possible to raise a significant amount of money *before* you ever need to hire your first development staff member. Also, consider how this system works. The strategy I'm unfolding here is something that can be taught to future team members, so they can produce the same results. Imagine the impact your organization can have and the reduction of overhead you'll have if everyone can manage a larger number of relationships!

Activating a Donor Before the Ask
As you review your cultivation list, you'll want to watch for those that haven't made a gift in nine or ten months. As they slip into these months, you'll want to shift them from the cultivation list to the activation list. From here, you can take the following steps in order to intentionally warm up the relationship before the renewal date arrives.

You can do this in a few ways:

1) **Intentionally ramp up your contact with them.** Now that they're on the activation list, you'll want to make sure you're making contact often over the next month or two.

Text messages, calls, emails, and invites to lunch should happen often. These are NOT times to ask. These are times to strengthen the relationship and inform them of the great things that are happening. Use casual conversation here, not a presentation. Keep things loose.

PRO TIP: *Ask about what is going on in your donor's life—like a good friend should. Avoid jumping right into what is happening with your work. This is a "warm-up" of the friendship, not a presentation for funding.*

---

2) **Look for ways to spend longer periods of time together.** Do they golf? Have a favorite restaurant? Can you invite them to a community event? By this time, you should know what they are passionate about and be looking for ways to invite them to participate in such activities. This is the time that you want to help them remember why they are friends with you in the first place.

3) **Invite them to serve at one of your events.** Imagine that you haven't spoken to Frank in many months, but his renewal date is about three months out. You move him to the activation list and begin looking for ways to spend more time with him. An easy conversation to have, especially if Frank is someone who has supported your work in the past, could be a simple text message like this:

Hey, Frank, you've been on my mind lately, so I thought I'd check in to see how you're doing. How are the kids? Is Suzy enjoying her new job? I noticed on Facebook you just returned from Europe. Was that work or vacation?

Never make an ask to volunteer in the same text message you are using to catch up. Send something like the above, and once Frank responds, use a few minutes to get caught up. Then, you might say something like this:

I'm so glad to hear you all are doing well; it's been so busy over here for us. But, it's a good kind of busy. You've probably seen that our golf tournament is coming up, and I'm almost finished gathering volunteers. One area in which we still need some help is check-in. Today it hit me—My friend Frank might want to help! Would you have some interest in helping out for about an hour? I would love to catch up. Plus, this would be a huge help if you are available. I'll even feed you a good lunch!

If your relationship with Frank isn't on the text-message level, and you need to call instead, I suggest calling only to catch up first. Then, a few days to a week later, make a follow-up call with the conversation mentioned above.

Activating a donor before the ask will protect you from being "that" friend. Don't get in a hurry with the funding. Remember that it's friendship first; the funding comes afterward. Then, during the activation process, look for ways to warm up the relationship, and remind your friend why they've supported you in the past and especially why they became your friend in the first place.

Make sure each relationship is warm, and you'll not only keep more friends, but you'll also create more lifelong donors for your organization.

CHAPTER 6

SOLICITATION: MAKING THE ASK

YOU CAN'T DO THIS ALONE

I have two adult children. When they were young, we would dress them, brush their teeth, comb their hair, and even put on and tie their shoes. We did everything for them. But, around age five, something strange happened. They started wanting to do things themselves. Suddenly, they didn't want Mom and Dad tying their shoes; they wanted to do it themselves.

This independence only grew as they got older—as it does with all of us. Tying your shoes, combing your hair, and brushing your own teeth are things that we all should be able to do independently of anyone else's help. But what about situations where we CAN'T do it by ourselves?

Too many times, we take our independent nature and carry it into situations where we clearly need someone to help. Take funding your cause for example. You may have started your organization completely funding it yourself, but soon, the vision grew beyond what you could personally afford to fund. Now what? Maybe you enlisted the help of close friends and family, but the vision outgrew their ability to help as well.

Asking for help isn't easy. Especially when it involves asking someone to give you some of their hard-earned money!

> **Asking for help isn't easy. Especially when it involves asking someone to give you some of their hard-earned money!**

CONSIDER THE CONSEQUENCES

What happens if we don't ask? Obviously, we may never receive, right? If we don't receive the funding, what happens? As I've alluded to in other chapters, there are serious consequences tied to not being fully funded. Have you ever paused to consider exactly who the people are that will continue to suffer because of your unwillingness to ask for help to fund your mission? How many people would be helped if you could increase your funding by another $10, $20 or even $50k a year? What would it mean for the single mother, the orphan, the addict, or the elderly?

This is the motivation I want you to put in your heart as we talk about the next step in our process: Solicitation.

IDENTIFYING YOUR FEARS

Understanding the impact that increased funding can make on those you serve can be a strong motivator, but it doesn't remove the fear of asking. Did you know that asking someone for money seems to be one of the greatest fears for nonprofit professionals? Here are two reasons I believe this to be so.

You Don't Feel You Deserve It

If you come from an unhealthy environment when it comes to handling money, you may have what is commonly referred to as a "poverty" mentality. This is common when people were raised in a poor home or by a family member who constantly reinforced that there wasn't enough. The good news is that you can overcome this!

I've known many people, myself included, that come from backgrounds like this. However, when you begin to realize that there are many people out there who want to help—they only need to be asked—it will help boost your confidence. Another way to boost your confidence is to remind yourself who you are in the eyes of God and how important your mission is to helping His people. Why would God place this important mission on *your* heart and then leave you too broke to fulfill it? He has many people in the world who have the resources we need to help His people. It doesn't make sense, right?

You Fear Rejection

This is most likely the top reason that people fear asking others for money. Fundraisers begin to think that a no is a personal rejection, so they run from it. After all, who wants to be rejected?

Most likely, that fear of rejection is coming from something in your past. Maybe a failed relationship or abandonment by a parent has caused you to stand clear of any situation that might end in a NO.

But remember this: when you receive a no, the donor isn't rejecting you personally. Let that sink in. It might be a timing issue. They may have upcoming expenses, past financial problems, or a whole host of other reasons they can't help right now. Refuse to take the no personally. It's never personal.

> **Refuse to take the no personally. It's never personal.**

I'd like to challenge this fear further by asking you, "What is the absolute worst thing that could happen if the donor told you no?" Would they stop being your friend? Would they run and tell everyone they know, "Hey, you know that Jerod asked me for money the other day?" Would they avoid your calls for the next year? Think this out. Would someone who knows you need funding for your cause be shocked if you ask them to help? Absolutely not! In fact, if you're cultivating your relationships correctly, they will be wondering why you didn't let them get involved sooner!

The only situation I can think of where a potential donor would be offended by a solicitation is if you rushed the process or created a high-pressure situation. Otherwise, you probably have many friends right now who are just waiting for you to explain to them where they can help. So, get to asking!

OVERCOMING FEAR

Regardless of your level of fear, you can overcome it. Say it out loud now, "I can overcome this fear!" It begins with a very simple step that transcends fundraising. We see it work with professional athletes, musicians, and anyone else who must perform in front of people. It's called PREPARATION.

Being overprepared for anything—and I mean anything—ultimately reduces the anxiety associated with it. So, how can we be prepared to make an ask to a protentional donor?

I like to call this the "6 Ps" of fundraising preparation. Let's go back to our example of Frank. During the cultivation process, you're gathering information constantly and storing it in a way that you can remember it. Relationships are built stronger as we spend time with potential donors and learn about them. To prepare to ask Frank for a contribution, you'll want to consider the following:

Person

What kind of person is Frank? Organically, as you get to know Frank better by spending time with him, you should be able to determine such things as:

1) Personality type
   - Is Frank a feeler, or is he more analytical?

2) Lifestyle
   - Is he a family man?
   - Is he a driven businessman?
   - Is he a socialite or more of a recluse?
   - Is he a saver or a spender?

Passion

What is Frank passionate about? Passion, more than any other motivator, will usually determine how someone might want to get involved in your cause. Think about the following:

1) What does Frank like to talk about?
2) What clues did he give you about his passions?
3) Where did he ask more questions about your mission?

Potential

You should know Frank well enough by now that you can determine what level of potential he may have to help. Think back to previous conversations and situations.

1) Does he have young kids at home or in college? Kids are expensive! Especially those that are in college. Did he mention his little boy plays baseball on a traveling team? Cha-ching! Are his two girls attending an elite college? Cha-ching! If you've never heard Frank speak about a scholarship, most likely, he's working double time to make it work.

2) Is Frank an older gentleman? Retired from a high-paying profession? This usually means a larger amount of expendable income. Or is he young and seems to be overextended, as most young professionals are? Just because there are a couple of new cars in the three-car garage doesn't mean he has margin.

3) Does Frank live in a large house or a small one?

4) Did he ever mention or post on social media anything about a vacation home?

5) Does Frank own his own business? How large is the business? Is he the sole owner?

6) Is Frank a school teacher or from another similar field that typically doesn't receive the pay it deserves?

Project

What sort of project would Frank most likely fund?

1) Would it be more people-centered or construction? I've discovered that most people fall into one of these two categories. Some like to help with immediate heartfelt needs, like feeding the poor, while others lean more toward long-term projects like construction.

2) What line of work is Frank involved in? Sometimes this can help determine interest. For example, an engineer might typically be highly analytical and lean toward funding an ongoing construction project.

3) Does Frank want a large or small project to consider? This may be determined by how many, if any, contributions he's made in the past. If this is a first gift, be careful presenting

something that shocks him. The goal for a first gift is always to lead to future involvement. You don't want one donation; you want a lifelong partner!

Proposal

What kind of proposal is Frank expecting?

1) Is Frank expecting a formal proposal? Most business people and large funding organizations will expect this because they need to be able to pass the information on to their partners or boards. Making this presentation look as professional as possible is very important for this reason. When you aren't around, your presentation is representing you. Make sure it does a good job of communicating who you are.

PRO TIP: *ALWAYS give three options when it comes to a formal presentation being sent or left behind for others to review. Countless times, I've been presently surprised by the level of gift someone will choose when given options. But don't give more than three. Too many options will spur an "I need to think about it" or even a no. When people become overwhelmed, their default is always no.*

---

2) Is Frank a casual person who only needs a verbal ask and info on how to make the donation?
3) Is Frank a close friend and really just needs a well-crafted letter or email?

Place

Choosing the correct place to make the ask is crucial. Loud restaurants or even places where many people may know your donor are not good choices. A place free from distraction is always best. Which location is best for this particular ask?

1) At his home?
2) At your home?
3) Over lunch or coffee?

PRO TIP: *Show up early to the restaurant, and sit in a place away from everyone else. Take the seat that faces out into the restaurant, so your donor's back is toward the distractions. This will help them focus on the presentation.*

---

4) Your office?
5) Fundraising event?

PRO TIP: *Try your best to avoid their office unless it's a formal presentation. There are too many distractions.*

THE ASK

Now that you're armed with motivation and preparation, you're ready to make the ask!

A solicitation for funds can be made in a variety of ways. Fund-raising events, formal presentations, personal letters/emails, or my favorite: the one-on-one personal ask. I believe the personal face-to-face ask is the most powerful and effective. Experience has proven to me that looking someone in the eye when you explain the *why* before asking them to help creates an environment that produces genuine partnership.

That being the case, let's dive deeper into how to successfully make a personal, face-to-face solicitation.

The One-on-One Ask

Ask for permission: "Frank, you've asked me quite a few questions about our school expansion lately. As you know we've been working hard to get this project funded. May I present you with a specific way to help?" If you've gauged the situation correctly, he will say yes.

Start with Why

Even if you've given it to him before, tell your story. Help Frank *feel* how important this need is and know exactly whom it will impact. Don't get bogged down with details. Keep it heartfelt. This is a great time to share the story of someone you recently met who is in great need of this project. For example, "Frank, I recently met a mother named Judy. She told me that two of her children are walking five miles each day to school, and the two little ones don't attend school at all because they can't walk that distance. It was heartbreaking to see this mother cry over her children."

Answer His Questions Before He Asks

Your presentation should always include the following list before Frank has a chance to ask. He's already wondering about these things, so answering them helps to remove any objections he may have to helping.

1) **What is the problem?** "Frank, the closest school for many of these children is ten miles away, and the government has no plans to build one closer anytime soon. Sadly, the schools that are in the area have over sixty children in one classroom. We fear that many of these children are going to continue the cycle of poverty because they don't have access to a solid education."

2) **Who will this impact?** "There are over ten thousand children in this remote area of Rwanda. We've done the research and found that when this school expansion is complete, we'll be able to admit two hundred of them to our school! Reducing the distance many are walking and reducing class size for all the schools will be major benefits to these children and their families."

3) **How soon are you hoping to complete this?** "The Rwandan school calendar begins in October, but we'll need to start enrollment in August. Our goal, depending on our funding, is to have the expansion complete before May of next year to begin the process."

4) **Will my gift make a real difference?** "In order to meet the deadline I just shared, we must have \$___ of funding before the end of this month. That will help keep our planning on track to meet our goal. As you know, there are many things

that have to be done before construction begins. When this school is complete, it's going to impact over two hundred children, their families, and the other schools in the area by relieving the current educational pressure we discussed earlier. It's going to impact people like Judy—the mother I mentioned."

PRO TIP: *Divide the total project funding into chunks. These amounts can serve as goals for you to communicate to donors. When you tell a donor, "We need the funding before May of next year," there is no sense of urgency for them. However, sharing smaller, time-sensitive goals will help them follow through and not get hung up with the larger number of the total funding needed. Large project numbers can intimidate donors into thinking their smaller gifts won't make a difference.*

Ask with Confidence

This is the million-dollar question! "Frank, I know you'll agree that this is an important need, and you've shown an interest in helping. Would you feel comfortable helping these children (not helping *us* or helping *me* but helping *the children*) with a gift of $___?" Then, STOP TALKING! Do not say another word— no matter how long the pause is. Make sure Frank can see (your facial expressions) and feel your concern about this need during this pause.

If Frank says, "YES, I could help at that level," you will obviously be elated and thank him. You'll let him know just how timely this is for your mission. Don't forget to indicate how you're going to get things in motion right away. This communicates to Frank the urgent need and how ready you are to put his donation to use right away.

If Frank says, "NO, I can't," the verbiage here is important. Remember: you asked him, "Would you feel comfortable with a gift of $___." This is VERY intentional because he may say no. If that happens, your response is a gentle, "I understand completely. I want this to be right for you. What level would you feel comfortable with?" Then comes the pause again. Let him process it without any input. What you just did was completely remove "no" as an option.

Make It Easy

We're going to assume Frank committed to some level of partnership. After you've thanked him and repeated the impact the gift is going to make, your next question will then be, "Would it be convenient if I stop by your office tomorrow at 10 a.m. to pick up that check? Whom should I connect with once I arrive?" Professionals are usually busy people. They will have an assistant handle the gift from this point, so it's important to know who that is and their contact information.

If he says, "No, I'll just mail you a check," you'll want to inform him that you will send a letter with an envelope to make things easier for him. You can also have the letter ready at the meeting with the amount of the gift already indicated. If Frank doesn't do that amount, it's easy to quickly adjust the amount and mail it to him the same day.

PRO TIP: *Mail it immediately! Emotion has a shelf life. This means every day that goes by, the fire you created in Frank is slowly dying.*

Solicitation Follow-Up

It's always a good idea to have a reason to follow up with him in about a week (the time it should take to know if he really sent a check). Ask like this, "Hey, what are you doing next Monday? Want to join me and some friends for golf?" If you don't have this type of relationship with Frank, you can simply ask, "Frank, I appreciate your willingness to send that check for funding. Would it be ok if I follow up with you in about a week to answer any further questions you may have?" Remember: this step is to provide some accountability for Frank to send the check. People are busy, and they can easily forget.

Solicitation can be scary, but when you remember why you're asking and come prepared, you'll soon be raising more money than you ever dreamed was possible.

Solicitation can be scary, but when you remember why you're asking and come prepared, you'll soon be raising more money than you ever dreamed was possible.

CHAPTER 7

APPRECIATION: GOING BEYOND THE STANDARD "THANK YOU"

Y ou've just received a generous donation!

Several months back, you were introduced to Frank. You had a great conversation and figured out a reason to stay in touch. You follow the Million Dollar Method system, and Frank begins moving through your donor pipeline and is soon cultivated into a true friend. A few months later, you make a great presentation to Frank, and he makes his first donation. You thank him verbally as he slides a check across the table. Is this the end? Is your work finished at that point? No!

> ## Did you know that one of the top reasons donors stop giving is because they feel the gift was not needed?

Did you know that one of the top reasons donors stop giving is because they feel the gift was not needed? Why do they feel this way? Because most organizations don't properly appreciate them!

While this is tragic, it also means that ANY extra effort you put forth in this area will leave your donor pleasantly surprised.

BE MEMORABLE

Saying, "Thank you," is customary. Most fundraising professionals know the importance of this, but few do enough to truly help the donor feel appreciated. Donors are familiar with getting a verbal thank you—maybe an email or even a card. These things are good but also very forgettable, and that's a problem.

If you want to separate yourself from others and build lifelong donors that feel great about supporting your cause year after year, don't just show your appreciation. Help them FEEL APPRECIATED in a way they won't forget!

Remember this: donors feel nothing from a thank you. However, when they feel appreciated, it makes them feel like family! It's time to move on from the old standard thank you and start helping our partners truly feel appreciated.

ABOVE AND BEYOND

Appreciation goes beyond a standard thank you. It says, "Your gift was needed, timely, and vital to the people we are trying to help through our mission." Appreciation says, "We couldn't have done this without your help." Appreciation helps your donor move from a transaction mindset to a partnership mindset. And, if you handle it correctly, they may become your biggest advocate for the cause.

MAKING IT STICK

So, what does it take to help someone feel appreciated? I've listed a few foundational principles below, but understand that this list is not exhaustive. Secondly, it's important to remember that appreciating a donor doesn't have to happen only after a contribution. Donors can and should be appreciated throughout the entire year. How can you respond to make this happen?

> **Donors can and should be appreciated throughout the entire year.**

Quickly

I can't express how important this is. I'm not talking about a few days; I'm talking about hours or even minutes. If someone makes an online gift, my goal is to give them a call while they still have the donation page of our website up. I can't tell you how many times I've called people only minutes after they made their online donation. Set systems in place to ensure that EVERY donor is appreciated QUICKLY!

Thoughtfully

If you've done your homework, you know the donor well and are able to tailor the appreciation to the way they like to be appreciated. Everyone has a love language! Speak their language when extending appreciation. The more personalized you can make your appreciation, the more longevity you get from it.

Appropriately

Your appreciation should make the donor feel like they are the largest donor you have—but don't overdo it. If the donor makes a large gift every quarter, you don't need to send a gift every time. However, don't let them fall off the appreciation radar just because they are a regular donor.

Here are a few specific ways I've appreciated donors in the past:

1) **Gifts**—We love sending gifts to our donors. Build up a stock of these things, so you're ready to appreciate a donor right away.
   - Branded clothing
   - Branded keychains or day planners
   - Food, sweets, or flowers delivered to their home or office. There are services that will even put your branding on the box.

PRO TIP: *Delivering something to the office will generate a buzz and create an opportunity for your donor to talk about your work to coworkers.*

- Handmade items made by those you serve. This has been a big hit for our organization. Our donors have loved receiving these things. A simple thing like a small bracelet can become a memento that donors keep for years.
- Thank you cards written BY those you serve. This isn't the standard thank you that you may write. When a donor receives a thank you from the people whom their gift helped, it becomes a powerful reminder of how important their giving is.

2) **Events**—This is a great way to show appreciation while at the same time deepen the relationship. If someone has made a sizable donation, you could invite them to join you at an NBA game, dine at a classy five-star restaurant, or even attend one of your special fundraising events. Be sure to emphasize that their invitation comes with no strings attached. A few things that we've used with success:
- Professional sporting events
- Private hunting events
- A round of golf with you at a high-class course
- Concert

3) **Trips**—If the gift was truly a major gift, you might consider paying for the donor to go visit your work personally. For example, our organization works in Rwanda, Africa. We've paid for several donors to come to see the work firsthand. Not only do they feel appreciated, but they also become a much stronger partner, having met those you serve.

4) **Video**—We use this a lot for our corporate or church partners. Recently, we had a church partner that funded a month
of food for an entire school in Africa. So, what did we do?
We put together a sixty-second video of the children eating
and laughing with a small personalized thank you from me
at the end. If you keep it short and produce it really well,
pastors will show the video to the entire congregation. Talk
about generating momentum!

I'm not suggesting here that saying "Thank you" in a handwritten
note or by phone call is not needed. I'm merely suggesting that
you take the thank you to the next level by packaging it with
something like the above mentioned items. Don't be fooled into
thinking that your handwritten thank you card alone will help
the donor feel appreciated.

> **Appreciate your donors well, and you'll
> be on your way to cultivating friends that
> support your cause year after year.**

Finally, I would encourage you to use this system to appreciate
EVERY donor—regardless of the gift size. This will help you
keep your heart humble and also protect your fundraising efforts
from losing a major donor who may have started small just to see
how you handled the gift. There have been countless times that

I've appreciated a donor properly to find that they were a *major* donor in disguise.

Appreciate your donors well, and you'll be on your way to cultivating friends that support your cause year after year.

CHAPTER 8

CELEBRATION: DRIVING HOME THE IMPACT A GIFT HAS MADE

EVERYONE LOVES TO CELEBRATE

When I was a child, there was a place that we all dreamed of having our birthday celebrations. This place had video games, foosball, bowling, a ball pit, and all-you-can-eat pizza! Every year, a friend would mention their birthday was coming up, and I secretly wished it would be at this incredible place.

Everyone loves to celebrate! The birth of a child, the marriage of a young couple, birthdays, retirements, and other significant events are important to people. So, what do we do? We celebrate with them! No one wants to celebrate alone during happy times, yet many fundraisers allow this to happen to their donors all the time.

CELEBRATING ALONE IS DEPRESSING

Much like the celebrations mentioned above, when a donor donates to your work, it is a significant event in their lives. Many hear about your cause and sacrifice their hard-earned money to help. When people do something for someone else, like donate to a good cause, it brings a slight dopamine hit to their system.

This means that if you've handled the relationship correctly, your donor will have a wonderful sense of joy afterward. They had a wonderful sense of happiness for helping those in need. Many secretly wish they had someone to celebrate with them because of the feeling it generates. They may tell a friend or family member, but that excitement begins to fade over time. That's why it's so important to celebrate with your donors!

CELEBRATING CREATES MOMENTUM

Making the celebration a priority helps you in many ways. First, it communicates what I like to call "What your gift did." Countless times, I've had donors tell me they discontinued their support to other organizations because they never knew what became of the project that they helped support. How disrespectful is this? Extremely disrespectful! Secondly, by properly celebrating with your donors, you're providing another dopamine hit to their system. It helps them relive the feeling they received when they first made the donation, but this time, it's even greater because they are seeing the impact for themselves! Thirdly, when they receive your celebration update, most will immediately share it on social media and with their friends, giving your cause even more momentum.

Your goal in your celebration communication is to say, "Your gift made a huge impact!"

WE'VE ALL ATTENDED BAD CELEBRATIONS

We've all been there. You're invited to a celebration, and soon, you realize that the organizers did not plan well, and people are not having a good time. Good celebrations do not happen by accident. They are intentional and thought out in a way that helps everyone feel at home. Good celebrations create an environment that causes people to anticipate returning for the next one. Donors are no different. Celebrating with a donor in an exciting way helps them anticipate when and how they can help again very soon!

PUTTING IT ALL TOGETHER

By now, you're starting to understand how the Million Dollar Method system works. You've created your identification, qualification, cultivation, activation, solicitation, and appreciation lists. Now, you're going to add the final step in this donor pipeline: Celebration. After a gift is made, and you've done a good job of helping the donor to feel appreciated, you'll slide them over to this final list. They will remain on this list for as long as it takes for you to complete the project they contributed to.

This list serves as a placeholder for you to remember to update them often on their project. If they've contributed to a long-term project like construction, you'll want to review this list often to send updated photos and even videos of how their project is progressing. If they've helped with a general donation, you'll want to circle back in a week or so with several photos of the work you've been doing recently. These celebration communications are the visual side of their donation. Remember: this is where you're proving to them that their contribution was well worth it and directly impacting the lives of people in a big way!

PRO TIP: *NEVER let a donor move from the celebration list until you've sent them a photo or video of where their giving has made an impact.*

If you have a good team or set of volunteers, this is a great place to get them involved. Explain the importance of capturing all the work you are doing and the power of sending regular visual celebrations to the donor. Put systems in place to ensure you're gathering photos and video at every event, outreach, food distribution, etc. These aren't just for your newsletter; these are for the personal celebration follow-ups you're now going to be doing.

KEYS TO MAKING THIS WORK

Plan Accordingly
Remember: good celebrations take planning and thought. Think through creative ways to send your celebration communications. Develop a system that works for you, so you never forget to check your celebration list. For example, I use the "Follow-Up Fridays" approach. Each Friday, I do my best to review our celebration list to ensure there are none that are lingering. If I can add a quick text message just to say, "Hey Bill, just wanted to say *Happy Friday*

and shoot you a quick photo of the foundation going in for the classroom you helped fund."

Make It a Priority
This step is the icing on the cake that most organizations will not take. Don't let this be you! The donor isn't properly moved through your pipeline until this step is taken, so make it a top priority.

Start Where You Are
Many fundraisers make excuses about not having camera gear or other items, but I would challenge you to start where you are, or you'll stay where you are. At this point, donors aren't necessarily looking for polished videos. The occasional raw cell phone video or photo of the project's progress is enough to show them their partnership is important to you.

Make It Personal
I've said this in other chapters, but this is important in *all* we do. The more personalized our communication with donors becomes, the deeper the relationship will become. For example, in the organization I lead, donors have the opportunity to purchase a goat for an impoverished family. We've set a system in place where that information gets routed to our team in the field immediately. They quickly deliver the goat to the family and take a photo of them standing in front of it. This photo is then sent back to our team in the US, so they can send it to the donor ASAP. We've even had the families hold a sign that says, "Thank you, Bill and Susan." Our turnaround goal is seventy-two hours! More times than not,

we hear donors say things like, "Wow! No organization has ever followed up like this. How impressive!"

Celebrating "what your gift did" with a donor is what separates you from all others in nonprofit work. Very few are doing this, and of those who are, there is rarely a system to remind them to do so. That's where the Million Dollar Method is different. By following through on sending your donors regular celebration communications, you'll be creating true partnership. Donors will soon be spreading the good work you're doing to their friends, which gives you the opportunity to add others to the pipeline.

Remember: no one wants to celebrate alone. So get out there, and start celebrating with your donor family!

CONCLUSION

WHERE TO GO FROM HERE

This strategy is a "Moves Management" system. Each day, your job as a fundraising professional is to move donors forward (at the right pace) into the next appropriate category. Then, when the donation is received, you've appreciated them, and finally, celebrated with them, you'll move the donor back to the cultivation list. This will be a never-ending process. Your job now becomes to move donors through and feed donors into the pipeline. As much as you do this, you'll soon have a growing organization that is raising the funding you need and beyond.

Regardless, if you're just getting started in the fundraising world or starting to realize that your current fundraising model isn't working, this Million Dollar Method will help you raise more money. It worked for me to raise over $7M over the last few years because I now have a process to maintain hundreds of relationships at a time. But, there is an added benefit of this system: you can teach it to others.

As your organization grows, you'll be adding other fundraising professionals to your team. They, too, need a framework to guide their relationships. This strategy can be adopted as an organizational model for everyone in your development department to use. Think of it this way. As you personally reach your threshold of donors to manage, you can add another person to your team and teach them this system. Then, when they are reaching their capacity, you add another and then another. Soon you'll have a team of fundraising professionals that have a clear strategy to build, maintain, and, best of all—RETAIN—relationships.

Retention is the key to growing the kind of lifelong donors your organization needs, and The Million Dollar Method helps you do just that. Constantly seeking the next new donor, then the next, then the next is exhausting. However, when you spend more of your energy on retaining the donors you already have, they will become the biggest champions of your cause. Then, they will be the ones bringing others into the pipeline.

Remember this: "A second gift from a donor is not only cost-effective but also an indication that they believe in your organization and support your cause enough to continue giving."[9]

Don't delay. Start using The Million Dollar Method today, and you'll have all the funding you need for tomorrow.

Implementing this strategy and navigating the many challenges that come with growing an organization can feel overwhelming at times. I remember this feeling very well. With over twenty years of nonprofit and business experience, there have been countless times when I simply did not know how to proceed. One of the

---

9 Ronald Pruett, "Are You Asking for a Second Gift?" 4aGoodCause, 20 June 2022, https://4agoodcause.com/are-you-asking-for-a-second-gift/.

best decisions I ever made to help me through these times was to hire a professional coach.

> **Don't delay. Start using The Million Dollar Method today, and you'll have all the funding you need for tomorrow.**

Today, I'm more productive and have more clarity than ever before. Advocates for Africa is growing rapidly, my personal life is in order, I'm eating healthy, and even going to the gym on a regular schedule. I attribute it all to hiring a professional coach to help me remove the clutter from my mind, provide accountability, and encourage me to keep striving to reach my goals.

In fact, coaching has so radically transformed my life that I became certified as a coach, so I could help others do the same. One of the greatest joys of my life is helping people live at their full capacity. When they do, their families, businesses, nonprofits, and the world benefit.

If you are looking for a sounding board or someone to help push you to achieve more, please reach out to me. I look forward to working together to change the world!

I'm now on a mission to help raise $1billion annually through the nonprofits I coach. If you are looking for a sounding board or someone to help push you to achieve more, please reach out to me. I look forward to working together to change the world!

9 781959 095781